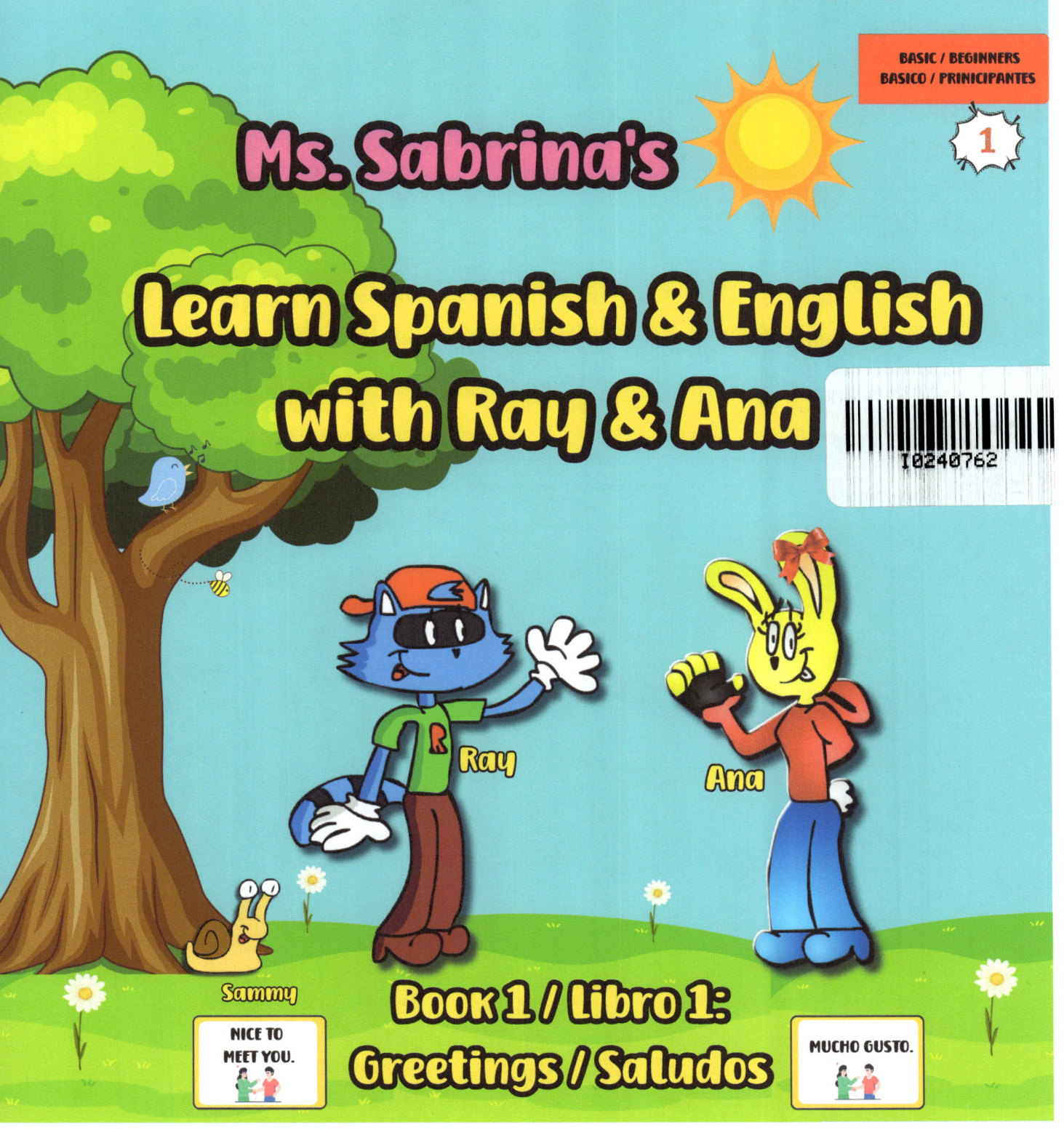

To my loving husband, children, parents, and sister, you are the pillars of my world. Thank you for your unwavering support. With boundless gratitude, I dedicate this book series to each of you, and to my dear niece Lia, the inspiration behind Ms. Sabrina. Your love, encouragement, and belief in me have fueled my dreams and creativity. Your presence in my life is a constant source of strength and inspiration, and I am profoundly grateful for the immeasurable blessings of your love and support. I love you with all my heart and soul.

To my students, thank you for teaching me countless lessons that go beyond the classroom. To those struggling to learn a new language, you are capable. I hope to be able to take away your fears and worries, as these books instill in you the confidence to see how easy it truly can be to learn a language.

Finally, I extend my heartfelt gratitude to my teacher and mentor, Ms. Elizabeth Flores for your invaluable mentoring, support, and inspiration. Your guidance, pearls of wisdom, honesty, sense of humor, and patience have been instrumental in shaping this journey, and I am deeply grateful for your lifelong presence in my life. To my talented illustrator and nephew, Jairo Puelles Pola, I extend my sincerest thanks for allowing me to incorporate your Oscar's Worlds characters into this book. Your creativity and skill bring these pages to life, and I couldn't be prouder to showcase your remarkable talents. I love you both.

It is my hope that these books contribute a small light to the world by blending learning with joy, and offering practical, meaningful tools that children and families can use every day.

Sabrina

Mentoring

Ms. Elizabeth Flores

ms.flores2020@yahoo.com
Credentialed Teacher

Story by

Sabrina Isabel Sánchez

@mssabrinasbilingualplaytime
@backtothebasicsandlivebeyond
https://backtothebasicsandlivebeyond.carrd.co/
MsSabrina.com

Illustrations

Jairo Puelles Pola

IG: @animacionespola
https://www.youtube.com/@animacionespola
https://www.youtube.com/@supersmilepower-lz5cn

For interactive learning with the book, watch Ms. Sabrina's videos on YouTube.

Para aprender de forma interactiva con el libro, mira los videos de Ms. Sabrina en YouTube.

YouTube.com/
@MsSabrinasBilingualPlaytime

https://MsSabrina.com/

Copyright © 2024 by Sabrina Isabel Sanchez
Author: Ms. Sabrina
Imprint: Back to the Basics & Live Beyond Publishing

Social Media:
Instagram/Facebook/YouTube/TikTok:
@mssabrinasbilingualplaytime / @backtothebasicsandlivebeyond
Website: MsSabrina.com
Email: sabrina@mssabrina.com
Website: backtothebasicsandlivebeyond.carrd.co
Email: backtothebasicsandlivebeyond@gmail.com

Mentoring by: Ms. Elizabeth Flores
Email: ms.flores2020@yahoo.com

Illustrations / Drawings by: Jairo Puelles Pola
Instagram: @animacionespola
YouTube: https://www.youtube.com/@animacionespola
https://www.youtube.com/@supersmilepower-lz5cn

First edition:
Originally published under ISBN 979-8321791097 on April 4, 2024.

Second edition:
Re-published under ISBN 979-8-9914099-0-2 on September 11, 2024.

All rights reserved.

No part of this publication may be reproduced, distributed, or transmitted in any form or by any means, including photocopying, recording, or other electronic or mechanical methods, without the prior written permission of the publisher, except in the case of brief quotations embodied in reviews and certain other non-commercial uses permitted by copyright law.

For permission requests, write to the publisher at backtothebasicsandlivebeyond@gmail.com.

This book is protected under copyright law.

Welcome to Book 1: Greetings

Thank you for selecting our beginner's book series to introduce your child to basic Spanish. Spanish stands as the fourth most spoken language worldwide, boasting the second-highest number of native speakers.

Exposing your child to a second language early on offers a multitude of advantages. It not only enhances cognitive abilities and cultural awareness, but also opens doors to future academic and career opportunities. Additionally, second language acquisition fosters vital communication skills and aids in overall brain development, giving your child a competitive edge in our interconnected global society.

Presented in a comic book format, Book 1: Greetings, featuring Ray and Ana, will guide your child to learn how to greet others in part one. Alongside these lessons, in part two, they will dive into concepts like different times of the day, manners, days of the week, and weather expressions. This book also emphasizes the development of social skills, interactive engagement, and self-expression. We are confident you and your child will find this initial adventure both enjoyable and educational.

Happy learning!

Bienvenido/a al Libro 1: Saludos

Gracias por seleccionar nuestra serie de libros para principiantes para introducir a su hijo/a al inglés básico. El inglés es el primer o segundo idioma más hablado en el mundo, dependiendo de cómo se mide.

Exponer a su hijo/a a un segundo idioma desde temprana edad ofrece una multitud de ventajas. No solo mejora las habilidades cognitivas y la conciencia cultural, sino que también abre puertas a futuras oportunidades académicas y laborales. Además, la adquisición de un segundo idioma fomenta habilidades vitales de comunicación y contribuye al desarrollo cerebral en general, brindándole a su hijo/a una ventaja competitiva en nuestra sociedad global interconectada.

Presentado en formato de cómic, el Libro 1: Saludos, protagonizado por Ray y Ana, guía a su hijo/a para aprender a saludar en la primera parte. Junto a estas lecciones, explorarán conceptos en la segunda parte como diferentes momentos del día, modales, días de la semana y expresiones relacionadas con el tiempo. Este libro también enfatiza el desarrollo de habilidades sociales, la participación interactiva y la autoexpresión. Estamos seguros de que usted y su hijo/a encontrarán esta aventura inicial tanto agradable como educativa.

¡Feliz aprendizaje!

HOW TO USE THIS BOOK

When reading this book, Ray's English phrases are in red, and Ana's Spanish phrases are in blue. At the bottom of the pages, you will see color-coordinated flashcards corresponding to the phrases and questions. These flashcards demonstrate how easily you can put the words together to form questions and phrases in both languages. Additionally, you'll find these flashcards, along with Ray and Ana puppets, at the back of the book, allowing you to practice at home or school. Finally, there are practice questions at the end of the book for further review. Have fun acting them out with the cutouts of Ray, Ana, and Sammy, and the flashcards.

CÓMO USAR ESTE LIBRO

Cuando leas este libro, las frases en inglés de Ray están en rojo, y las frases en español de Ana están en azul. En la parte inferior de las páginas, verás tarjetas didácticas con código de color que corresponden a las frases y preguntas. Estas tarjetas muestran lo fácil que es combinar palabras para formar preguntas y oraciones en ambos idiomas. Además, encontrarás estas tarjetas, junto con marionetas de Ray y Ana, al final del libro, lo que te permitirá recortarlas y practicar en casa o en la escuela. Por último, hay preguntas de práctica al final del libro para repasar. Diviértete actuando con los recortables de Ray, Ana y Sammy y las tarjetas didácticas.

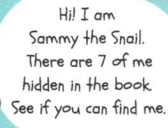

Hi! I am Sammy the Snail. There are 7 of me hidden in the book. See if you can find me.

Examples

Please refer to back of book for Sammy's Quotes in Spanish and English.
Consulta la parte trasera del libro para ver las citas de Sammy en español e inglés.

Ejemplos

Part / Parte 1:

Greetings
Saludos

Part / Parte 2:

Daily Greetings
Saludos Diarios

Days of the Week
Días de la semana

Magic Words
Palabras Mágicas

Weather
Tiempo

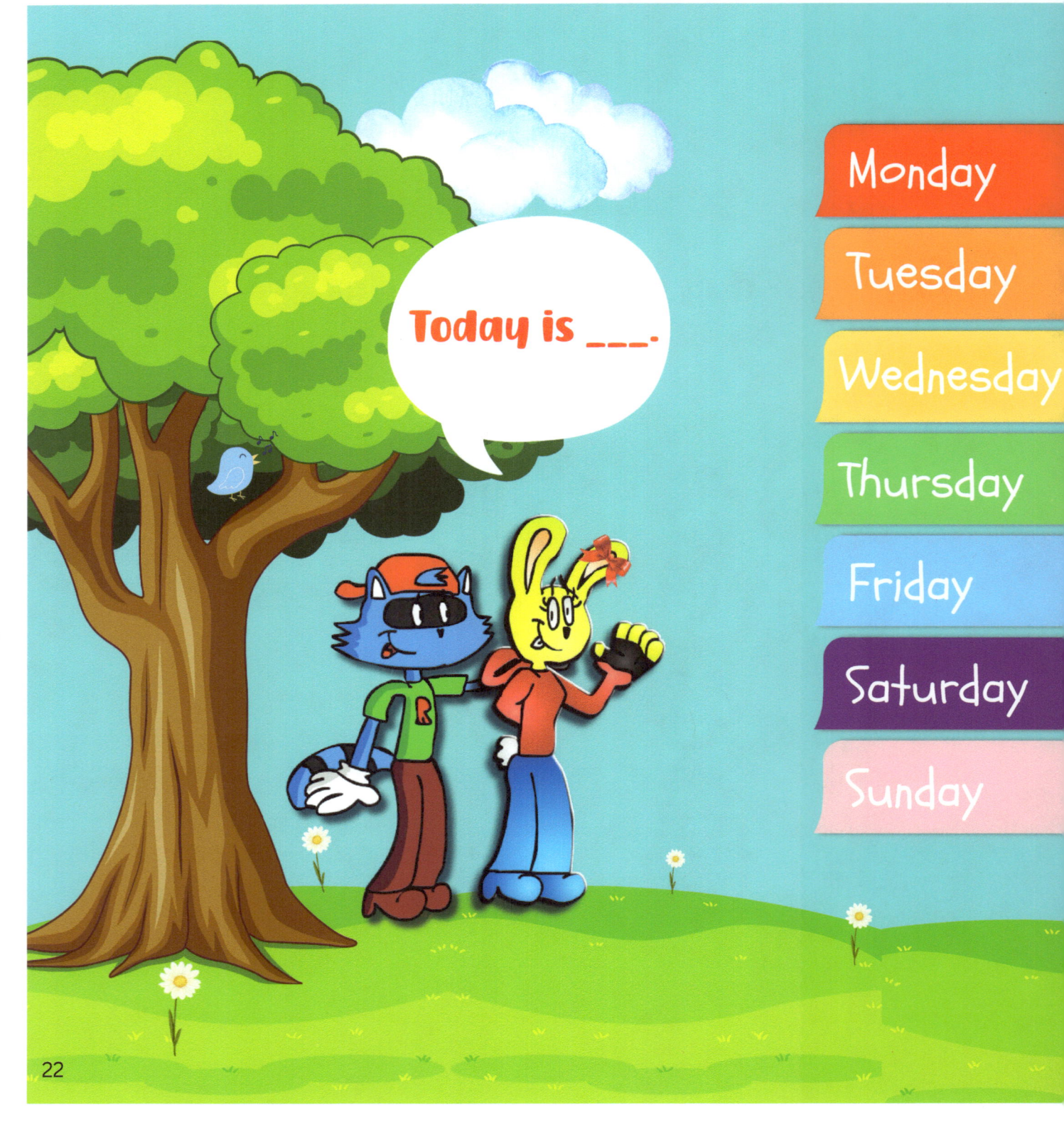

Part / Parte 3:

Questions
Preguntas

Flashcards
Tarjetas Didácticas

Puppets
Marionetas

 **Sammy's Quotes**
Citas de Sammy

Questions / Preguntas

Practice in Spanish

Practice a short dialogue with the Ray and Ana Puppets, where they ask each other in English and Spanish:

Hello.
What is your name?
Where are you from?
How are you?
Do you speak English?
Do you speak Spanish?
What day is it?
How is the weather?
Goodbye.

Practicar en inglés

Practica un diálogo breve entre las marionetas de Ray y Ana, donde se preguntan en inglés y español:

Hola.
¿Cómo te llamas?
¿De dónde eres?
¿Cómo estás?
¿Hablas inglés?
¿Hablas español?
¿Qué día es?
¿Cómo está el tiempo?
Adiós.

 HELLO	 WHAT IS YOUR NAME?
 HOW ARE YOU?	 MY NAME IS ___.
 I AM FINE.	 WHERE ARE YOU FROM?

Cut out
recortar

GOOD MORNING

MONDAY

GOOD AFTERNOON

TUESDAY

GOOD NIGHT

WEDNESDAY

LUNES	BUENOS DÍAS 
MARTES	BUENAS TARDES 
MIÉRCOLES	BUENAS NOCHES 

THURSDAY

SUNDAY

FRIDAY

YES

SATURDAY

NO

Cut out
Recortar

DOMINGO	JUEVES
SÍ 	VIERNES
NO 	SÁBADO

Cut out
Recortar

Cut out
Recortar

HAY NUBES 	**HACE SOL** 
ESTÁ LLOVIENDO 	**HACE VIENTO** 
HACE FRÍO 	**HACE CALOR** 

Sammy's Quotes

Pg.	ENGLISH	ESPAÑOL
2	Hi! I am Sammy the Snail. There are 7 of me hidden in the book. See if you can find me.	¡Hola! Soy Sammy el Caracol. Hay 7 como yo escondidos en el libro. Intenta encontrarme.
9	"The world is full of kind people. If you can't find one, be one." –Nishan Panwar	"El mundo está lleno de personas amables. Si no puedes encontrar una, sé una." –Nishan Panwar
15	"A person's a person, no matter how small." –Dr. Seuss	"Una persona es una persona, no importa lo pequeña que sea." –Dr. Seuss
21	"Small acts can make a big difference." –Unknown	"Pequeños actos pueden hacer una gran diferencia." –Anónimo
25	"A kind word is like a spring day." –Russian proverb	"Una palabra amable es como un día de primavera." –Proverbio ruso
27	"Be silly, Be honest, Be kind." –Ralph Waldo Emerson	"Sé tonto, sé honesto, sé amable." –Ralph Waldo Emerson
30	"Friends are like cookies; you can never have too many." –Unknown	"Los amigos son como las galletas; nunca puedes tener demasiados." –Anónimo
Back / Atrás	"Slowly, but surely." –Unknown	"Sin prisa, pero sin pausa." –Anónimo